To: James and Amelia
Happy Easter

Love you so much
oxoxoy

April 21, 2019

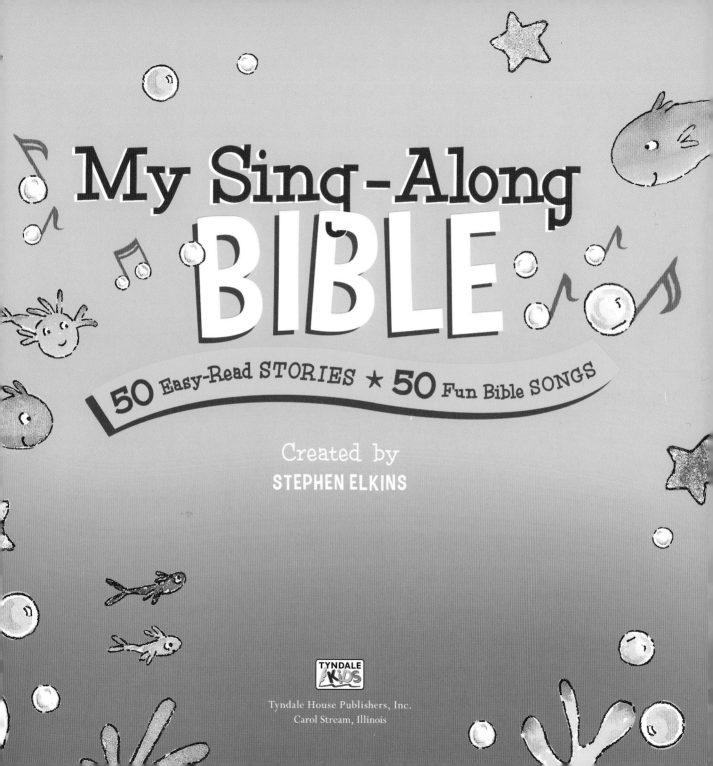

My Sing-Along BIBLE

50 Easy-Read STORIES ★ 50 Fun Bible SONGS

Created by
STEPHEN ELKINS

TYNDALE KIDS

Tyndale House Publishers, Inc.
Carol Stream, Illinois

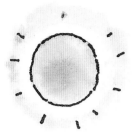

Who made the oceans, so deep and wide?
Who made the sun to rise every morning?
Do you see the flowers and clouds?
I see a baby and a bee a-buzzing!
I wonder, "Who made these wonderful things?"
The first words in the Bible tell us. God made them all!

Who Made Me?

In the beginning God created the heavens and the earth. GENESIS 1:1

God Created

In the beginning, oh, in the beginning! (4x)
In the beginning God created the heavens and the earth. (4x)
We sing the glory of God
In the beginning, oh, in the beginning!
We praise His name!
Lift Him high above creation
Because He created it all!

God told Noah to build an ark. Noah obeyed!
God led His animals to the ark. Elephants and zebras, monkeys and giraffes came. Then it rained for 40 days and nights. The earth was covered with water! But God kept Noah's family and the animals safe inside the ark.

Noah and the Flood

Noah did everything exactly as God had commanded him. GENESIS 6:22

No. No. Noah!

Boom, boom! How the thunder was crashing.
Zoom, zoom! How the lightning was flashing!
No, no, Noah did not fear.
Boom, boom, for the Lord
Our God was near.

LITTLE LESSON:
God is in control!

Let's Sing

The rain stopped falling! But the ground still had to dry. So Noah waited inside the ark. He sent out a dove and hoped it would find dry land. The dove came back with a leaf from an olive tree. Hurray! The land was dry. God had saved them!

The Dove Returns

This time the dove returned to [Noah] in the evening with a fresh olive leaf in its beak. GENESIS 8:11

Who Built the Ark?

Who built the ark? Noah! Noah!
Who built the ark?
Brother Noah built the ark.

LITTLE LESSON: Our God is a saving God!

No one can count how many stars there are.
But God told Abraham to try. God promised him,
"You will have more people in your family than the stars you see!"
That's more than a million! Could it be true? Yes!
God kept His promise and a nation was born!

Abraham's Promise

The LORD took Abram outside and said to him, "Look up into the sky and count the stars if you can. That's how many descendants you will have!" GENESIS 15:5

The Lord Is Faithful

The Lord is faithful to all His promises.
The Lord is faithful to all His promises
And loving toward all He has made,
And loving toward all—He forgave.
Oh, the Lord is faithful to all His promises.

LITTLE LESSON:
God always keeps
His promises!

An Egyptian princess went down to the Nile River.
There she saw something very strange.
A tiny basket was floating along the riverbank.
What a surprise to find a baby boy inside!
But this child would become God's special helper!
She named him Moses.

Baby Moses in a Basket

The princess named him Moses, for she explained, "I lifted him out of the water."
EXODUS 2:10

You Will Keep Us Safe

O Lord, my Lord, You will keep us safe.
You will protect us.
O Lord, my Lord, You will keep us safe.
You will protect us.
You will keep us safe and watch over us
In our coming and going forever.
O Lord, my Lord, You will keep us safe.
You will protect us. (4x)

Let's Sing

LITTLE LESSON:
God will keep you safe!

Balaam was riding his donkey.
Suddenly the donkey went off the road.
It had seen an angel!
But Balaam couldn't see it.
He grew angry and struck the donkey.
The poor donkey cried out! "Why are you hitting me?"
Balaam was shocked!
God can even make a donkey talk!

Balaam's Donkey

The LORD gave the donkey the ability to speak.
"What have I done to you that deserves your beating me three times?" NUMBERS 22:28

Is Anything Too Hard?

Is anything too hard for the Lord?
Is anything too hard for the Lord?
There is nothing He can't do.
Have a little faith, believe it's true,
And you will find there's nothing He can't do.

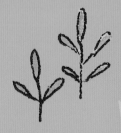

Let's Sing

LITTLE LESSON:
God can do all things!

11

Joshua led God's people to a city called Jericho.
A big wall stopped them from going inside.
God told Joshua's army
to march around it for seven days.
On the last day, all the people would shout.
They obeyed. And when they shouted, the wall came down!
God's ways aren't like ours!

Joshua's Shout

Shout! For the LORD has given you the town! JOSHUA 6:16

Joshua Fit the Battle of Jericho

Joshua fit the battle of Jericho,
Jericho, Jericho.
Joshua fit the battle of Jericho,
And the walls came tumblin' down.

Let's Sing

13

A family is something special.
God created the first family!
Adam and Eve showed us what a family should be like.
First there is a mommy and a daddy.
Then God may give them special blessings called children!
I hope your family serves the Lord each day!

God Created Families

As for me and my family, we will serve the Lord. JOSHUA 24:15

My Family Matters

My family matters, my family matters,
It matters to me.
My family matters, my family matters
Because I believe.

LITTLE LESSON:
God created
my family!

15

Naomi and her family moved to a faraway land.
There Naomi's husband died.
Naomi's sons married Ruth and Orpah.
Then Naomi's sons died too.
She decided to go home to Bethlehem.
Ruth said, "Wherever you go, I will go.
Your God will be my God."
Ruth was a wonderful friend!

Ruth and Naomi

Wherever you go, I will go; wherever you live, I will live. Your people will be my people, and your God will be my God. RUTH 1:16

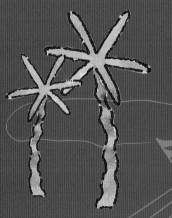

Where You Go

Where you go, I will go.
Where you stay, I will stay.
And your people will be my people,
And your God will be my God.

Let's Sing

LITTLE LESSON:
Good friends take care of each other!

Hannah was sad. She didn't have any children.
So she prayed, asking God for a son.
She promised God that her son would be His friend.
God said YES! Hannah had a baby boy named Samuel.
Just as Hannah promised, Samuel was God's
friend and served Him his whole life.

Hannah's Gift

O LORD . . . if you will look upon my sorrow and answer my prayer and give me a son,
then I will give him back to you. 1 SAMUEL 1:11

You Answered Me

In my distress, I called to the Lord,
Called to the Lord, called, O called.
O in my distress, I called to the Lord,
And He answered me.

Let's Sing

19

Goliath was a giant.
He said mean things about God's people.
David faced him and said, "Your sword is your power.
MY power comes from God!"
David was brave! He threw a stone at Goliath
with his sling, and down he came!
There is power in the Lord's name!

David and Goliath

You come to me with sword, spear, and javelin, but I come to you in the name of the LORD of Heaven's Armies. 1 SAMUEL 17:45

The Name of the Lord

The name of the Lord is a strong tower.
The righteous run into it and are safe.
The name of the Lord is a strong tower.
The righteous run into it and are safe.
The righteous run into it and are safe.

Let's Sing

LITTLE LESSON:
There is power in the name of the Lord!

God decided to take Elijah to heaven.
His friend Elisha made a request.
"Give me twice the faith of Elijah!"
The answer would be "yes" if Elisha
saw him leave. Suddenly a chariot
took Elijah up into heaven! Elisha watched him go.
God gave Elisha a double blessing of faith!

Double Blessing

If you see me when I am taken from you, then you will get your request. But if not, then you won't.
2 KINGS 2:10

The Song of Blessing

The Lord bless you and keep you now.
The Lord make His face to shine upon you
And be gracious, and be gracious,
And be gracious unto you.

Let's Sing

LITTLE LESSON:
It takes a big God
to give big blessings!

23

Queen Esther heard about an evil plan. God's people would be hurt! Esther asked all the people to pray. She invited the king to dinner. There she told him about the evil plan. "Save us!" she cried. And he did! God had made Esther queen at just the right time!

Queen Esther

Who knows if perhaps you were made queen for just such a time as this? ESTHER 4:14

For Such a Time as This

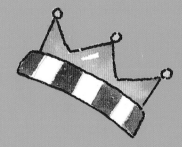

For such a time as this,
God brought us here to sing.
For such a time as this,
We lift our voice and sing.
Praise Him, O praise Him,
Praise our Lord and King.
For such a time as this,
God brought us here to sing.

Let's Sing

LITTLE LESSON:
God's timing is always perfect!

25

David was a shepherd boy. Shepherds care for sheep.
David thought, "People are like sheep. And God is like a
great Shepherd. He cares for us!" So David wrote a song.
It praised the Lord for being his wonderful Shepherd.
Like a shepherd, the Lord gives us everything we need!

The Lord Is My Shepherd

The LORD is my shepherd; I have all that I need. PSALM 23:1

The Lord Is My Shepherd

The Lord is, the Lord is my shepherd. (3x)
How 'bout you? Yes, He is!
The Lord is like a shepherd, He knows what to do.
The Lord is like a shepherd, He'll walk with you.
The Lord is like a shepherd, He knows what to do.
When His little lambs are tired, He'll help them through! (2x)

LITTLE LESSON:
God is our Great Shepherd!

27

God is strong and mighty!
David said God was his "hiding place."
Like a shell around a turtle, the Lord is our shield.
We can ask Him to protect us from trouble.
But even if trouble comes, God will help us through it.
God is our strong hiding place!

My Hiding Place

You are my hiding place; you protect me from trouble. PSALM 32:7

You Are My Hiding Place

You, You are my hiding place.
You will protect me from trouble all my days.
You, You are my hiding place.
You will protect me, O my Lord.

Let's Sing

29

Our Father in heaven loves us! He gives us good things.
He watches over every step we take and helps us do the right thing.
That is what it means to "walk by faith."
We trust the Lord to care for us and show us
what to do each day.

Walking with God

The LORD directs the steps of the godly. He delights in every detail of their lives. PSALM 37:23

Come Walk with Me, Lord

Come walk with me, Lord.
Come talk with me, Lord.
Come stay with me, Lord.
Come say to me, Lord,
That I will be Yours
And You will be mine.
Come live with me, Lord, always.

Let's Sing

LITTLE LESSON:
God walks with us along the way!

"Shhhh!" the little boy said. "We need to be quiet.
We don't want to wake up the little birds!"
Sometimes it is good to be quiet. David wrote another song
that tells us to rest quietly and enjoy what God made.
God is truly great, isn't He?
Shhhhh!

Be Still and Know

Be still, and know that I am God! PSALM 46:10

He Will Quiet You

He will quiet you! (2x)
He will quiet you with His love, His love!
Oh, He will quiet you!
He will quiet you!
He will quiet you with His love, His love!
O God!

Let's Sing

LITTLE LESSON:
It's good to be still and think about God!

33

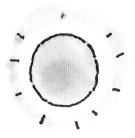

Prayer is talking to God.
What should you talk to God about?
The Bible teaches us to pray about everything.
If a friend isn't well, pray! If your puppy is sick, pray!
Nothing's too big or small for God.
So pray about everything!

Pray about Everything

All the animals of the forest are mine. PSALM 50:10

All Creatures of Our God and King

All creatures of our God and King
Lift up your voice and with us sing
Alleluia, alleluia.
Thou burning sun with golden beam,
Thou silver moon with softer gleam,
O praise Him, O praise Him,
Alleluia, alleluia, alleluia.

Let's Sing

35

David took care of his father's sheep.
That's because sheep aren't very smart.
They need help finding food or a drink of water.
So David guided the sheep each day.
But who guided David? The Lord!
He will guide you, too. Just trust Him like a little lamb!

God Is Our Guide

You guide me with your counsel. PSALM 73:24

The Lord Will Guide You

The Lord will guide you.
He will take care of your need,
Take care of your need.
The Lord will guide you.
He will take care of your need,
Take care of your need.

GOD'S WAY

LITTLE LESSON:
God always knows the way!

Angels are God's invisible helpers!
They watch over us and keep us safe from harm.
They also deliver messages to people. Mary was visited by an angel who told her she would be Jesus' mother. Just think—an angel is watching over you right now!

Angels Watchin' over Me

[God] will order his angels to protect you wherever you go. PSALM 91:11

Angels Watchin' over Me

Day is dyin' in the west,
Angels watchin' over me, my Lord.
Sleep, my child, and take your rest,
Angels watchin' over me.

Let's Sing

LITTLE LESSON: Angels watch over us and keep us safe!

Why do we thank God at mealtime?
He has given us food! How?
He created the tiny seeds planted in the ground.
He sends rain and they grow! Some grow into peanuts, and some become grapes. Now we can make peanut butter and jelly sandwiches! Praise Him!

The Lord Will Supply

The eyes of all look to you in hope; you give them their food as they need it. PSALM 145:15

God Is Great

God is great and God is good.
Bless the Lord, bless the Lord!
And we thank Him for our food.
Bless the Lord with me.

Let's Sing

LITTLE LESSON:
God gives us
food every day!

41

Sometimes we hurt on the outside . . .
sometimes on the inside.
We're sad and our hearts ache!
God's friend Jeremiah had an aching heart.
God's people were doing bad things,
so God was taking away His favor.
But then Jeremiah got some happy news!
God would soon comfort them, inside and out!

A Comfort for All

I will turn their mourning into joy. I will comfort them. JEREMIAH 31:13

God Will Comfort You

As a mother comforts her child, so will God comfort you. (2x)
He will turn your sadness to gladness,
Sadness to gladness.
"I will turn your sadness to gladness.
I will give you joy."

42

LITTLE LESSON:
God's love brings us great joy!

43

Prayer is like talking on the phone.
We can't see the person we're talking to.
God's friend Jeremiah tells us that God listens to our prayers.
When we pray, God promises to answer.
And He answers in a way we CAN see! So keep on praying!

Prayers Will Be Answered

Ask me and I will tell you remarkable secrets you do not know. JEREMIAH 33:3

He Will Answer

Call on God and He will answer,
He will answer by and by.
Call on God and He will answer,
He will answer from on high.
Call on God and He will answer
And tell you great and wonderful things.
How gracious He is! How gracious He is!
How gracious He is, so call upon the Lord.

Let's Sing

45

God gives us blessings.
Blessings are good things that bring us joy!
Ezekiel said God's blessings would be like drops of rain falling from the sky.
How many raindrops fall? A thousand . . . maybe a million!
God's blessings will be more than we can count!
What a mighty God!

Showers of Blessing

There will be showers of blessing. EZEKIEL 34:26

Showers of Blessing

There will be showers of blessing falling on you,
Showers of blessing falling on you, (2x)
So let the blessings fall.
Showers of blessing falling on you, (3x)
So let the blessings fall.
Showers of blessing falling on you,
So let the blessings fall.

LITTLE LESSON:
God will send showers of blessings!

47

Ezekiel had the strangest dream!
He saw a valley filled with dried-up bones! God asked,
"Can bones live again?" Ezekiel said, "Only You know!"
God answered, "Tell them they will live!"
Ezekiel obeyed. Suddenly he heard a loud noise.
The bones came to life! Everything is possible with God!

Dry Bones

Can these bones become living people again? EZEKIEL 37:3

Dry Bones

Dem bones, dem bones, dem dry bones, (3x)
Now hear the Word of the Lord.
O, Ezekiel connected dem dry bones, (3x)
Now hear the Word of the Lord.
Dem bones, dem bones gonna walk around, (3x)
Now hear the Word of the Lord.

Let's Sing

LITTLE LESSON:
All things are
possible with God!

49

What an awful law! King Darius said, "No more praying!"
When Daniel found out, he just kept on praying.
The king's helpers saw him, and they put him in a lions' den!
But Daniel wasn't afraid. He just kept on praying.
And God answered! He sent an angel to save Daniel!

Daniel and the Lions

My God sent his angel to shut the lions' mouths. DANIEL 6:22

Three Times a Day

Three times a day
He got down on his knees, yeah, yeah.
Three times a day
He got down on his knees, yeah, yeah.
He got down and prayed and prayed,
Giving thanks to God, I say.
Three times a day, three times a day,
Three times a day Daniel prayed, yeah, yeah.

50

Let's Sing

LITTLE LESSON:
Pray no matter what!

51

It was a simple command: "Go to Nineveh!"
But Jonah didn't want to!
He got on a boat and sailed away from God.
Soon a storm came. Jonah was thrown into the sea!
A giant fish swallowed him! Jonah prayed, "I'm sorry, Lord."
The fish spat Jonah out. This time Jonah obeyed!

Jonah and the Big Fish

Get up and go to the great city of Nineveh. Announce my judgment against it. JONAH 1:2

Who Did Swallow Jonah?

Who did, who did, who did, who did,
Who did swallow Jo, Jo, Jo, Jo . . . ?
Who did swallow Jonah, who did swallow Jonah,
Who did swallow Jonah down?

LITTLE LESSON: It's good to obey God the first time!

Why do we pray on our knees?
It's a way of honoring God.
It says that God is greater than we are.
It says God is always good, and we are not.
Kneeling is our way of showing God we are humble.
It shows on the outside how we feel on the inside!

A Humble Heart

Walk humbly with your God. MICAH 6:8

Walk Humbly with Your God

He has shown you, O man, what is good. (2x)
And what does the Lord require of you?
To act justly, to love mercy,
To walk humbly, to act justly.
That is what the Lord requires of you.

Let's Sing

LITTLE LESSON:
We kneel before God to show humility!

55

Mary and Joseph went to Bethlehem.
Baby Jesus would soon be born.
They couldn't find a place to stay!
What would they do?
God knew!
He led them to a tiny stable.
There Jesus was born! The King would sleep in a
feed box for animals called a manger.

A Manger for the King

[Mary] gave birth to her first child, a son. She wrapped him snugly in strips of cloth and laid him in a manger. LUKE 2:7

Cradle Hymn

How much better thou art attended
Than the Son of God could be
When from heaven He descended
And became a child like thee.

Let's Sing

When Jesus was born, a new star appeared in the sky!
Wise men from far away knew something wonderful had happened.
A king had been born! That king was Jesus.
This star would lead them to the King. So they followed the star.
Soon they found Jesus and worshiped Him!

Behold That Star

Where is the newborn king of the Jews?
We saw his star as it rose, and we have come to worship him. MATTHEW 2:2

Behold That Star!

Behold that star, behold that star up yonder.
Behold that star, it is the star of Bethlehem.
There was no room found in the inn . . .
It is the star of Bethlehem.
For Him who was born free from sin . . .
It is the star of Bethlehem.

Let's Sing

LITTLE LESSON:
It is wise to seek Jesus!

Jesus grew up. One day, He was walking by a lake.
He saw two brothers fishing. Jesus said, "Come, follow me!
I will show you how to fish for people." What did He mean?
Jesus meant He would show them how to share
the Good News that God forgives!

Come, Follow Me

[Jesus said,] "Come, follow me, and I will show you how to fish for people!"
And they left their nets at once and followed him. MATTHEW 4:19-20

Come, Follow Me

Come, follow Me, and I will make you fishers of men. (4x)
We will catch them with our kindness,
We will catch them with the love of God.
We will catch them with our kindness,
And bring them to the Lord.

60

LITTLE LESSON:
Jesus wants us to follow Him!

61

Matthew was Jesus' helper.
He wrote down the things Jesus said and did.
As Jesus taught about prayer, Matthew wrote down His words.
Today we call it the Lord's Prayer.
"Father in heaven, may Your name be kept holy.
We hope Your Kingdom comes soon.
And let Your will be done!"

The Lord's Prayer

Our Father in heaven, may your name be kept holy. MATTHEW 6:9

The Lord's Prayer

Our Father in heaven, hallowed be Your name. (2x)
Your kingdom come, Your will be done
On earth as it is in heaven.
Your kingdom come, Your will be done
On earth as it is in heaven.

LITTLE LESSON:
We can pray t
our Father lik
Jesus did!

62

Let's Sing

Jesus told His followers not to worry.
"Look at the birds! God takes care of them.
He gives them plenty to eat!"
Worry isn't a good thing.
We must learn to trust God.
He promised to take care of us.
We are worth much more to God than little birds!

Look at the Birds

Look at the birds. . . . Your heavenly Father feeds them.
And aren't you far more valuable to him than they are? MATTHEW 6:26

Seek First

Seek first, seek first,
Seek first His Kingdom.
Oh, ya gotta seek first,
Seek first, seek first His Kingdom
And His righteousness.

LITTLE LESSON:
Give your
worries
to God!

Let's Sing

Wise children read their Bibles.
Then the words turn into actions!
It's like a smart person who builds a house on a big rock.
When the storms come, the house doesn't fall down!
When you see rain, remember to be wise
and build on the Rock called Jesus!

Build on the Rock

Though the rain comes . . . and the winds beat against that house,
it won't collapse because it is built on bedrock. MATTHEW 7:25

The Wise Man Built His House upon the Rock

The wise man built his house upon the rock.
The wise man built his house upon the rock.
The wise man built his house upon the rock,
And the rains came tumbling down.

64

LITTLE LESSON:
The Bible makes me wise!

65

Many people came to see Jesus.
At dinnertime, they were hungry.
But there was only a little bit of bread and a few fish.
Then Jesus did something only He could do.
He blessed that food, and 5,000 people ate dinner!
A little in Jesus' hands goes a long way!

Jesus Feeds a Big Crowd

He took the seven loaves and the fish, thanked God for them, and broke them into pieces.
MATTHEW 15:36

After Giving Thanks

Then Jesus took the seven loaves, (clap, clap, clap)
Then Jesus took the little fish, (clap, clap, clap)
And when He had given thanks,
He broke them, He broke them.
And when He had given thanks,
All did eat.

Let's Sing

LITTLE LESSON:
A little. when given to Jesus. becomes a lot!

Jesus' helpers had made a mistake.
They thought only grown-ups should come to Jesus.
They tried to stop children from visiting!
But Jesus loved the children. And the children loved Him, too!
"Let the children come," He told them.
"Heaven is filled with people who have
faith like these children!"

Let the Children Come

Jesus said, "Let the children come to me. Don't stop them! For the Kingdom of Heaven belongs to those who are like these children." MATTHEW 19:14

Jesus Loves the Little Children

Jesus loves the little children,
All the children of the world.
Red and yellow, black and white,
All are precious in His sight.
Jesus loves the little children of the world!

Let's Sing

LITTLE LESSON:
Jesus loves little children!

69

Jesus could heal sick people fast!
We call that a miracle!
But our bodies are made to heal slowly when we're hurt.
It's important to know that all healing, fast or slow, comes from God above.
Doctors and nurses can help us heal.
But God makes all healing possible!

The Great Doctor

Jesus healed many people who were sick with various diseases. MARK 1:34

I Will

I will, I will, I will restore you to health.
I will, I will, I will heal your wounds.
I will, I will, I will heal my people.
I will, I will let them enjoy abundant peace.

Let's Sing

LITTLE LESSON:
God is the Great Doctor who heals our bodies!

71

Jesus and His helpers left the crowds behind.
They got into a boat, and suddenly a storm came up!
His helpers were afraid. Jesus was sleeping!
"Wake up!" they shouted. "We may drown!"
Jesus got up. "Quiet!" He said. The storm stopped!
Even the wind and waves obey Jesus!

Jesus Calms the Storm

[Jesus] rebuked the wind and said to the waves, "Silence! Be still!" Suddenly the wind stopped, and there was a great calm. MARK 4:39

The Wind and Waves Obey Him

Even the wind and the waves obey Him!
Even the wind and the waves obey!
The raging sea stirs until
The voice of the Lord makes it still.
Will He help me? Yes, He will! (Yes, He will!)
'Cause even the wind obeys.

LITTLE LESSON:
Even the wind and waves obey Jesus!

Jesus is called the Good Shepherd.
That's because He always knows the way!
The Bible says WE are like lambs.
We don't always know what to do.
So we run to Jesus!
He is kind and shows us the way.
The Good Shepherd cares for His lambs!

Little Lambs, Come to Jesus

I am the good shepherd.
The good shepherd sacrifices his life for the sheep. JOHN 10:11

I Am the Good Shepherd

I am the Good Shepherd.
I am the Good Shepherd.
And the Good Shepherd
Lays down His life for the sheep.

Let's Sing

LITTLE LESSON:
Little lambs, come to Jesus!

75

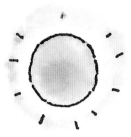

Jesus loves me. How do I know?
The Bible tells me so!
He loves me when I'm good.
He still loves me when I'm not so good.
When I win, He celebrates with me!
When I lose, He comforts me.
What time does Jesus love me?
All the time!

Jesus Promises to Love Me

This is how God loved the world: He gave his one and only Son. JOHN 3:16

Jesus Loves Me

Yes, Jesus loves me!
Yes, Jesus loves me!
Yes, Jesus loves me!
The Bible tells me so.

Let's Sing

LITTLE LESSON:
Jesus loves me all the time!

Jesus showed us how to love.
LOVE is an action word!
It's not always easy to show love.
That's because you must DO something!
Like helping a friend, or visiting someone who is sick.
The love Jesus teaches us about is an "action" love.
It always helps others!

Love One Another

Love each other. Just as I have loved you, you should love each other. JOHN 13:34

Love One Another

"Love one another," I have read.
"Love one another," Jesus said.
"As I have loved you,
So must you love one another."

"Love one another"

LITTLE LESSON: Love always does something good for others!

79

Do you want to be a good friend?
Jesus taught us how!
He said, "Love other people the way I have loved you."
Jesus was patient and kind. Jesus was a helper.
To be a good friend, do what Jesus did!
Jesus said, "You are my friends if you do what I command."

Jesus Is My Friend

You are my friends if you do what I command. JOHN 15:14

A Friend Loves at All Times

Oh, a friend loves at all times!
Oh, a friend loves at all times!
Morning, noon, or night,
A friend is a delight,
For a friend loves at all times!

Let's Sing

LITTLE LESSON:
Loving others makes us a friend of Jesus!

Jesus died on a cross.
He died so that we might live forever in heaven!
Then Jesus was put in a tomb.
A large stone was rolled in front of it.
Later, two women came to visit.
Surprise!
Jesus was not inside!
An angel said that He had risen.
Jesus is alive!

Jesus Is Alive

He isn't here! He is risen. MATTHEW 28:6

Risen Indeed!

Risen, He has risen, He has risen, allelu, allelu! (3x)
He is not here,
He has risen indeed.
I believe, O I believe.

82

Let's Sing

LITTLE LESSON:
Jesus is alive!

83

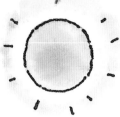

Paul sailed to faraway places.
He was a brave missionary.
He told people the Good News about Jesus.
Many believed and became Jesus' followers!
Maybe you can't go to faraway places right now.
But you can still be a missionary right where you are.
Tell others about Jesus!

Paul the Missionary

Go into all the world and preach the Good News to everyone. MARK 16:15

Go!

Go into all the world
And preach the Good News to all creation.
Go into all the world
And preach the Good News to everyone.

LITTLE LESSON:
Be a missionary
right where you are!

85

It's good to talk with God each day.
He's your best friend!
God loves it when you spend time with Him.
Some people pray at bedtime. Others choose morning.
Find a time that's right for you. Then pray!
Ask the Lord for the things you need.
Prayer really changes things!

Prayer Changes Things

Pray about everything. Tell God what you need, and thank him for all he has done. PHILIPPIANS 4:6

Do Not Be Anxious

Do not be anxious about anything,
But in everything,
By prayer and petition,
With thanksgiving, present your requests to God.
And the God of peace will understand,
So take His hand.

Let's Sing

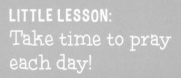

LITTLE LESSON:
Take time to pray
each day!

Remember Paul?
He left home to tell people about Jesus.
God always took care of him. He didn't run out of food.
Paul said that God was rich. God will provide for us, too!
He can supply all that we need . . . all of the time!

God Will Provide

God . . . will supply all your needs from his glorious riches. PHILIPPIANS 4:19

He Meets My Needs

Before I ask, my God meets my need.
Before I ask, my God meets my need!
Oh, He loves and understands me,
His gentle voice I hear before I ask.
He hears my need, oh, how He hears my need.
Oh, how He hears my need.

Let's Sing

LITTLE LESSON:
God will supply
all you need . . .
all the time!

89

Some days are great, when everything goes well.
Other days are not so good!
We don't know what tomorrow may bring.
But God is with us no matter what!
He is there to help us through good days and bad.
So let's be thankful God is with us every day!

Be Thankful Always

Always be joyful. Never stop praying. Be thankful in all circumstances.
1 THESSALONIANS 5:16-18

O Give Thanks

O give thanks unto the Lord,
For He is good, He is good!
O give thanks unto the Lord,
For His love endures forever.

Let's Sing

When we set a good example, we encourage others!
When you thank the Lord for your lunch,
your friends see your good example.
Even babies in high chairs may be watching you and learning!
And who sets the best example of all?
That's right . . . Jesus!

Set a Good Example

You yourself must be an example to them by doing good works of every kind. TITUS 2:7

Imitators of Jesus

Be imitators of God
As dearly loved children, children, children.
Be imitators of God
As dearly loved children, children, children.
And live a life of love, child,
Just as Christ loved us.

Let's Sing

LITTLE LESSON:
Set a good example
for others!

93

God promises to take care of us.
And He will keep that promise!
No matter where you are, God is with you.
Day or night, He will never leave you!
Whether you're with friends or in a tent by yourself,
God is there with you! God keeps His promises!

The Lord Is with Me Always

God has said, "I will never fail you. I will never abandon you." HEBREWS 13:5

God Will Be with You

The Lord your God will be with you
Wherever you go.
The Lord your God will be with you
Forever child—yeah!
The Lord your God will be with you
Wherever you go.
The Lord your God will be with you
Forever, child.

Let's Sing

LITTLE LESSON:
God will never leave you!

The Bible says Jesus stands at the door and knocks. He wants to come in.
Come into where? Our hearts and lives! He wants to be our Savior and friend.
"Knock, knock!" Do you hear Him? Open the door and let Jesus come into your heart!

Behold, I Stand at the Door

Look! I stand at the door and knock. If you hear my voice and open the door,
I will come in, and we will share a meal together as friends. REVELATION 3:20

Behold, Behold

Behold, behold, I stand at the door and
Knock, knock, knock. (2x)
If anyone hear my voice, if anyone hear my voice
And will open, open, open the door,
I will come in.

LITTLE LESSON:
Open the door and let
Jesus into your heart!

96

Let's Sing